I'm not sick. Society is!

ADD/ADHD is an adaptation to society - not an illness. A 5-step Drug Free Parent/Teacher Guide.

Jaydene Morrison, MS, LPC, NCSP, NCC

Bloomington, IN Milton Keynes, UK

authorHOUSE

AuthorHouse™
1663 Liberty Drive, Suite 200
Bloomington, IN 47403
www.authorhouse.com
Phone: 1-800-839-8640

AuthorHouse™ UK Ltd.
500 Avebury Boulevard
Central Milton Keynes, MK9 2BE
www.authorhouse.co.uk
Phone: 08001974150

First published by AuthorHouse   9/26/2006

ISBN: 1-4259-2029-2 (sc)

Printed in the United States of America
Bloomington, Indiana

This book is printed on acid-free paper.

PRAISE FOR *I'm not sick. Society is!*:

"Jaydene Morrison has made an important and practical guidebook for parents who have children others would diagnosis with the label ADHD, but which she so wisely calls the CIC – the creatively inspired child."

Leonard Shlain, MD
ChiefofLaparoscopic Surgery, California Medical Center
San Francisco

"At last I've found an easily understandable practical hands-on management guide that I can recommend for parents with ADD children, as an alternative to medication management."

Bruce A. Naylor, MD, FACP
Norman, Oklahoma

"You line out the necessary steps needed to help the child and the situation the child is in. I think you have a good book and the steps are good."

John Harris, DO
Fairview, Oklahoma

"I like very much the positive approach you have taken. I see it as providing hope to parents."

Robert Campbell, PhD
Director, Program Support and Development HDOE
Hawaii State Department of Education

"To treat (ADD) properly takes a lot of time and expertise – probably more time than most general private practice pediatricians are able to spend with a family...therefore the primary responsibility, again, is with the parents."

Doug Hardy, MD
Assistant Professor ofPediatrics and Internal Medicine, UT Southwestern
Dallas, Texas

THIS BOOK IS DEDICATED TO

Russ Peterson, *MA Education*

whose inspiration, creativity and
encouragement made this book possible.

Also, to the Steven Spielbergs, David Neelemans, Jeremys
and the others who have shown
the future to all of us –
especially to the light for my future:
my grandchildren
McKenna, Tyler, Maci Morrison and
university-bound Blair Morrison.

ACKNOWLEDGEMENTS

Creative inspiration from the following people
has made this book possible:
Sue Frederick, BrilliantWork; marketing designer, Gene
Malowany; Vicky Sama, editor;
friends Robin and Alice Ames and Laura Kugel
and Beverly Hayes; and the support of my family Jay, Kerri,
Mac and Lori Morrison.

CONTENTS

INTRODUCTION

"At the earliest moment we glimpse Man on earth, we find him moving at an accelerating pace. In our generation it is perhaps the most difficult and dangerous of all the current problems of the human race."

Arnold Toynbee

"The first step toward any solution of any problem is optimism."

John Baines

There is a heated national debate about what causes ADD. or ADHD.[1] Some experts argue that ADD is genetically inherited. Others say it's nothing more than children adapting to a changing society. The majority of educators believe ADD is a genetically inherited behavioral disorder causing children to perform in a dysfunctional manner. However,

"The fact that an opinion has been widely held is no evidence whatever that it is not utterly absurd."

Bertrand Russell

Analysis of Matter

---

[1] The Diagnostic and Statistical Manual of Mental Disorders – Fourth Edition (DSM-IV) refers to "Attention-Deficit Hyperactivity Disorder" as ADHD. ADHD has become shortened in the public domain as ADD. For the sake of brevity, we will refer to the condition being discussed in this book as ADD.

An Alternative to ADD Drugs

Who has the audacity to say your child is dysfunctional? The position in this parents'/teachers' management guide is that ADD children are **not** dysfunctional. Rather, they are physically and mentally alive individuals who are attempting to find creative ways of interpreting the massive amounts of "information sensation" that life hurtles at them. Clearly, one has to be super-human to digest even a fraction of the information in our technologically driven age. Michael Niman and P.W. Miller write in an Adbuster magazine article (2005), "By the time a child enters kindergarten they will have spent more time watching TV than a college student would have spent in class earning a college degree. By the time an American is 19 years old, they will have spent 11,000 hours in school and 19,000 hours watching TV."

The Scanning Minds

Observe an ADD child for a few hours on a typical day and you would likely find him or her watching cartoons and MTV and playing with "action" toys and video games at the same time. In many cases he or she is also munching on some advertised sugary food.

Some children are good "sorters" of information. They focus on what appeals to them. Others, those children called "ADD dysfunctional," are "scanners." They are trying to take it all in. They love the creative buzz of figuring out what to do with all of the information stimulation. They love activity and the related challenge of placing themselves in the middle of all the action. They are good at fast moving video games and sports—it suits their scanning minds. They're ready for action. These children are best equipped for analyzing masses of data because they have creative synthesizing minds.

Anick Jesdanum writes in the *Rocky Mountain News*, "With a few keystrokes, we'll be able to tap much of the world's knowledge."

So, where do we start dissecting the problem of determining why the "establishment" considers your child "ADD dysfunctional?"

One has to begin by asking what percentage of children in the United States educators diagnose with ADD characteristics. Numerous authorities contend that as many as 20% of school children supposedly have ADD. That means one out of five children may have it.

So, what is the apparent cause of this rapid increase in ADD children, when 10 years ago we never heard of it? Is it genetic, as some claim? If so, why has it just recently surfaced? This author believes it is a mental adaptation to present society and not dysfunctional behavior.

"Will all this instantly accessible information make us smarter, or simply more stressed?," asked Jesdanum. "When can we break to think, absorb and ponder all this data? It may take better technology to cope with the problems better technology creates." his article adds.

The challenge for all of us – especially the most creative in our midst – is to search for a thoughtful mental space between our thinking selves and our social selves, so we can fit in where we need to without giving up our creative souls.

In their book, *The Fourth Turning*, William Strauss and Neil Howe write, "The faster a society progresses, the more persistently generational issues seem to keep springing up. The more modern a society thinks itself, the more resistant its people become to legitimizing generational change as an *idea*. While modernity is about rational progress toward the future, generations stand as reminders of how much people remain tied to the subconscious vestiges of their past."
So, is ADD a gigantic national management problem or is it simply children adjusting to change? Who should take responsibility for it?

Is the Child Responsible?
Not really! Children at early ages are not even aware they are "dysfunctional" in that they do not "sense" they are acting differently than their peers.

Is the School Responsible?
Absolutely! But the school system seldom takes responsibility for social problems. In fact, these creative children who have already moved into the technological world are expected to retreat back to the 1930s-style classroom to learn. They have difficulty functioning in these antiquated classrooms. The school takes the easy

solution – it gives the children a "mellowing" pill or puts them in a special education class. These children are labeled as "misfits." So what must a concerned teacher do?

Is Society Responsible?

Perhaps. Our media-manipulated society is, in fact, one of the main causes of the problem. But the media doesn't take any responsibility. They are just trying to sell goods to the consumer. Television programmers and advertisers seldom consider the consequences of their actions.

Is the Medical Community Responsible?

The "typical" physician is indebted to the pharmaceutical industry. It is easier and quicker for the physician to prescribe drugs that the industry says will solve the problem rather than for the physician to get personally involved.

Is the Parent Responsible?

Absolutely, YES! Parents must take the ultimate responsibility for their children. No one else will!

This book is a simple guide to cultivate our ADD creative children. Parents who feel their child is not adapting to the home or school environment, not playing well with peers and not accepting basic parental guidance, may need to ask, "Is my child one of these 'impulsive' children." If the answer is "yes," attention-to-detail is necessary.

ADD-characterized children are little energy engines constantly seeking new routes to information analysis and application. By properly managing the typical Creatively Inspired Child, or CIC (the preferred term to ADD), parents must provide a nurturing environment for the child to blossom. Therefore, the goal of this book is to provide parents and teachers with sample management tools to create environments that will allow these children to **thrive** and realize their creative potential.

Symptoms for the CIC usually appear prior to the age of seven. Most parents first "discover" the child is CIC-inclined when the child begins school. The confining structure of the school accentuates the emotional entanglements with others. This is also the time of life when all children's minds are open to new possibilities, and yet, they find themselves in confining institutions or settings. How does the CIC work out a compromise between his or her unique visions and the restricted environment? That is the ultimate challenge of the CIC and parents and teachers—creating the compromise between the child's needs and society's directives.

Below is a simple list of questions that allows parents to evaluate whether or not their child fits the criteria outlined above. The questionnaire was compiled by Dr. Russell A. Barkley, author of *Attention Deficit Hyperactivity Disorder*, and Dr. George J. DuPaul, author of *The ADHD Rating Scale*, in an unpublished manuscript, the rights of which have been approved for reprinting in the public domain.

The method of scoring the "parent-insight diagnosis" is described on the next page.

Circle the number in the column which best describes the child.

	Not very much	Just a little	A lot	Very much
Often fidgets or squirms in seat	0	1	2	3
Has difficulty remaining in assigned area	0	1	2	3
Is easily distracted	0	1	2	3
Has difficulty waiting turn in groups	0	1	2	3
Often blurts out answers to questions	0	1	2	3
Has difficulty following instructions	0	1	2	3
Has difficulty sustaining attention to tasks	0	1	2	3
Often shifts from one uncompleted activity to another	0	1	2	3
Has difficulty playing quietly	0	1	2	3
Often talks excessively	0	1	2	3
Often interrupts or intrudes on others	0	1	2	3
Often does not seem to listen	0	1	2	3
Often loses things necessary for tasks	0	1	2	3
Often engages in physically dangerous activities without considering consequences	0	1	2	3

Total all columns.
(Total of columns 1 and 2 is always 0)   0   0   ____   ____

Total (columns 3 and 4)   _____

To score this test, simply add the number of all items that rated as two or higher. A total score of eight or more is the number for someone thought to be ADD (or CIC). This diagnosis is merely for preliminary screening purposes. If the score is above eight, you may also want a school or professional to test your child to confirm the diagnosis. Additionally, since many authorities say CIC behavior is inherited, you may also want to take the test to see how you score. You might be surprised!

So, what is a *"Creatively Inspired Child?"*
According to the DSM's classic definition, ADD symptoms include the following:

Step 1: THRIVING (Self-worth related issues)

A typical CIC child thrives to acquire self-worth by defending himself or herself against society's labels and reacts "dysfunctionally" by

- Arguing repeatedly with others
- Blaming others for their mistakes
- Becoming angry and resentful when given direction
- Becoming spiteful or vindictive about any guidance

Step 2: ORGANIZING (Structure related issues)

A typical CIC child seeks organization in life by desperately searching for meaning or structure by

- ➤ Resisting instructions
- ➤ Changing tasks before they complete the initial task
- ➤ Seldom organizing the environment satisfactorily or at all
- ➤ Losing things repeatedly

Step 3: MOVING (Environmental related issues)

A typical CIC child moves through life with "gusto" in order to experience as much as possible. Consequently, he or she

- ➤ Fidgets
- ➤ Is easily distracted
- ➤ Is drawn to action filled situations
- ➤ Regularly spills or drops things while attempting to manipulate them

Step 4: CONNECTING (Peer related issues)

A typical CIC child wants desperately to connect with others without overwhelming them, but enthusiasm gets in the way because he or she

- ➤ Has difficulty listening for an extended period of time
- ➤ Moves around while watching TV or movie when asked to focus
- ➤ Has trouble waiting a turn

➤ Is easily annoyed by competitors

Step 5: CREATING (Interpretation related issues)

A typical CIC child always seeks a unique answer to traditional problems by having

➤ Daydreams
➤ Difficulty focusing on structured tasks
  such as homework
➤ Spontaneous responses to answers before
  the question is completed
➤ Intrudes on others' conversations
➤ Outbursts of behavior

*Despite these "disruptive" responses to life, consider viewing the CIC from a positive perspective. The child's innovative behaviors and unique insights into our world enable him or her to become the **discoverers, explorers, inventors and leaders** of the future.*

"It isn't hard to be good from time to time. What's tough is being good every day."

Willie Mays

STEP 1

"Never do anything against your conscience, even if the state demands it."

Albert Einstein

Albert Einstein was a stellar ADD individual who applied his unique vision to analyze his changing world.

As this book has stated, many authorities believe CIC characteristics are inherited. Others believe the children are merely "adapting" to a changing social fabric. Dr. Elizabeth Koppitz, a leading psychologist and developer of the Koppitz scoring system for the Bender Gestalt Test, did a research study of Japanese children in Japan and in a California Japanese community. She found a completely different pattern between the two societies. The Japanese children in California were more hyperactive and unstructured in their approach to her test than the children living in Japan. Dr. Koppitz's research, and many others like hers', reinforces the thesis that a child's environment is one of the main causes of his or her hyperactivity.

Clearly, as a parent, you know your child better than the school, doctor, neighbors or other relatives. Take into consideration what others say, but do not completely rely on their opinions. Their opinions can possibly provide insights into your child's social interactions and serve as the foundation for developing a coping strategy. Teachers should not be influenced by the comments of other teachers or administrators either.

If your child's total score on the Parent Insight Diagnosis is eight or more, you should consider that he or she has already been negatively labeled by many adults in authoritative positions. Therefore, you may need to roll up your sleeves and get to work correcting the negative path your child is being pushed down.

The consequences of these negative labels are that your child is likely to be already **arguing** with others about these evaluations, **blaming** others for their mistakes rather than taking responsibility for them and already **resenting** anyone who puts them in the "dysfunctional box." In fact, your child could already becoming downright **vindictive by rejecting** any attempts to be controlled.

Just like adults, children have to feel loved in order to flourish. We all have to respect and accept ourselves to become survivors in this competitive world. Therefore, the goal for a parent of a CIC is to help him or her learn how to accept themselves by building their own sense of self-worth and unique version of how to **thrive** and realize their potential.

To truly excel, all children have to honor themselves and learn to value who they are—our duty as a parent is to see that this happens.

To begin building a unique identity for your CIC, consider the following ways to help him or her build a sense of self.

Visual Aids for Self-worth

Build an image gallery using the following:

➤ Photographs or videos of your child doing successful things

➤ Display the child's awards in the child's room

➤ Create positive valuation cards for family members, friends and peers to write upbeat things about your child. Have your child do the same for peers. In other words, get everyone to start thinking positively about his or her relationship with your child.

➤ Put all these "positive input devises" on the wall of the child's room or a coffee table book where it can be seen everyday. A bulletin board or refrigerator can also serve as display areas, as they typically do.

As the primary caregiver, a parent needs to help their CIC mentally put his or her arms around themselves so they can feel they can learn how to heal themselves. Though positive feedback needs to be the primary focus of your relationship with your child, you still need to acknowledge his or her negative behavior. Simply acknowledge your child's negative habits so that they can learn to understand the primary causes and move beyond them. Acknowledging past behavior can help your child identify "societal shortcomings" and help him or her learn new methods of behavior that will allow them to fit in and remain unique. Most importantly at this state of the game, by understanding your child's negative past behavior, parents can also begin developing positive ways of overcoming their own negative responses to their child's behavior.

To get down to the task of finding solutions for your child's intense emotional behavior, consider using the following Emotions Chart as a "route to the positive."

E M O T I O N S   C H A R T

Event _____

Emotion(s) felt _____

_____

People involved _____

_____

Place incident happened _____

Actions involved _____

_____

Trigger situation –or– event that started problem

_____

Consequence of behavior

_____

Potential solutions _____

_____

Future steps _____

_____

_____

*The **Emotions Chart** was filled out based on the following situation between two CIC youths.*

Sample Chart for Defining Emotions

Scenario #1: Zack was chasing Nathan on the playground. Zack tripped Nathan, and Nathan stumbled and began to cry. Nathan told the teacher, who then sent a note home to Zack's mother. When Zack's mother asked Zack why he tripped Nathan, Zack said Nathan was going to tell the teacher that Zack had his homework. Zack, in turn, said he didn't have Nathan's homework, but Nathan didn't believe him.

Initially, sit down and fill out the series of events of the Emotion Chart with your child. This helps children understand how to begin understanding the process.

Here is what Zack's chart looks like:

Event: Playing on the playground at school.

Emotion: Afraid
(Defining the emotion helps your child realize what emotions dominate his or her life.)

People: Friend
(This helps your child understand who friends and foes really are.)

Place: Playground.

Action involved: Tripped friend

(Helps your child define the primary response to conflict.)

Triggering situation: Friend accused him of something he had not done.

Consequence of behavior: Zack tripped a friend because he was afraid of getting into trouble.

Potential solution: Zack must ultimately come up with his own alternative behavior. There are options: Zack could explain to Nathan that he did not have his homework and explain why he reacted negatively. If this did not work, Zack could go to the teacher and explain that Nathan had lost his own homework. Zack could then ask the teacher's help in locating it.

Future step: Finally, the parent needs to help Zack evaluate his own solutions to help him avoid this situation in the future. Zack needs to practice creating his own problem solving behavior. Practice makes perfect. It may take many charts and months to change behavior but this is how we all learn through repetition.

Sample Chart for Realizing Limits

Scenario #2: Jason was playing a video game with his older brother Stephen. Stephen's friend was watching. Steven was winning. Stephen and his friend started laughing at Jason and called him a "dummy." Jason turned around and hit Stephen and then ran out of the room. Stephen began chasing him. Jason started yelling for his mother to come quickly because Stephen was going to beat him up.

Here's an example of Jason's chart:

Event: Brothers playing a video game at home.

Emotion: Anger.

People: Brother and friend.

Place: Home/family room.

Action involved: Video game competition.

Trigger situation: Losing game and brother and friend teasing him.

Consequence of behavior: Jason hit his brother and yelled for his mother to rescue him.

Potential solution: Stephen needs to take part of the responsibility. Jason, however, should come up with alternative explanations about how to react when being teased. Losing a competition and being teased are part of growing up. Jason's solutions include the following:

1. Do not play games with someone you know will seriously beat you and embarrass you or else play with them in a non-competitive or cooperative mode. A cooperative mode should be something you evaluate when the game is purchased.

2. Jason will verbalize his feelings to Stephen. For instance, he can say, "Stephen, it makes me feel

badly when you tease me. How would you feel if I teased you?" Relating his true feelings is important. Additionally, the parent could also have the brothers role-play the incident and develop a variety of response options.

Future step: Discuss how to stop and think before one leaps.

Creating a library of Emotion Charts can help parents develop problem-solving techniques. Filling out the charts will help you and your child evaluate his or her ability to solve his or her own problems. The parent may find that many of the child's conflicts occur in the same environments, at the same time of day, with the same people and involve a primary emotional response. The charts will give you and your child clues to aid in the development of a future that he or she, not others, manage. An unregulated CIC can create an internal tsunami that affects everybody around and puts him or her out of touch with themselves and others. Understanding the cause and effect of behavior patterns is the key to avoiding conflict.

An Emotion Chart needs to be filled out each time your child has strong emotional experiences such as excessive fear, extreme sadness, uncontrolled anger and inappropriate affection.

A copy of the Emotion Chart is located in the glossary for you to reproduce and use.

Self-analysis is really the best kind of medicine. The goal of charting is to help your child understand the emotional "triggers" that pushed him or her beyond acceptable behavior.

> *"Self-discipline begins with the mastery of your thoughts. If you don't control what you think, you can't control what you do. Simply, self-discipline enables you to think first and act afterward."*
>
> **Napoleon Hill**
> Author of *Think and Grow Rich*

Every child holds the key to his or her own survival. This awareness is the biggest challenge for the parents and teachers of a CIC. Practicing healthy emotional reactions over and over again can help your child build a positive future. There should be no limit to the number of charting events; practice makes perfect.

Documenting the whole process by placing the charts in a filing system according to emotional reactions will allow you and your child to have a problem solving "history" to evaluate as a means to personal success and overcoming failures. Periodically, reinforce the positive moments of this history with rewards for the best solutions. Rewards can be simple things such as big hugs and kisses. Simple rewards are often the best. Showing affection is essential to your child's self esteem.

An alternative approach:

Substitute "Oh Peanut Butter" in Place of an Angry Response

Another fun way of controlling a child's intense anger is to utilize humor. Consider the "Oh, peanut butter" option. There is nothing magical about the expression "peanut butter." Having your child come up with his or her own words or personal expression puts more control in their hands.

The next time someone says something to your child that elicits a strong emotion, tell him or her to look the other person in the eye and say, "Oh, peanut butter." When he or she sees the other person's response, tell him or her to avoid laughing, which would likely negate the effect of the response. This can be a phenomenally effective technique. It can completely disperse the anger response in both combatants. Here are some reasons why the "peanut butter" response is so powerful:

➤ It puts the power to control emotion within your child's grasp.
➤ It is an unexpected creative response.
➤ It totally disarms both individuals and causes a smile rather than a grimace on the faces of the combatants.

When all Else Fails, Consider Escaping or Withdrawing

> *"Timing is everything!*
> *Concentration and deep breathing*
> *are a way of stilling the mind and*
> *allowing a wide awareness and*
> *clarity of one's life to unfold."*

Russ Peterson

Since intense emotions are common for a CIC, your child may find situations where he or she cannot help but feel overwhelmed by a potential conflict. Help your child recognize there are occasions when the odds are against him or her and escaping is the best strategy. Fast legs are a solution! Strong, fearful emotions weaken a child's resolve and cause confusion about what to do. Strategic problem solving behavior is only possible when your child is calm, cool and collected, not feeling fearful. Please note that this solution is not an "escape-pass" for your child to avoid all issues in life but rather a way to make the right choices at the right time.

Once your child has left a conflict scene, he or she needs to go back to the charting process. Keep in mind that this can be done in the head, in the privacy of a bedroom, or with parents or teachers. Whether your child actually deals directly with the aggressive person or not depends on whether the other person is receptive to positive communications. Encouraging your child to ask for parental assistance is acceptable so long as it doesn't become a regular practice.

It is also important to remember that powerful emotions can be positive tools.

> *Anger, grief, fear—these emotional experiences are not negative in themselves; in fact they are vital for our survival. We need anger to define boundaries, grief to deal with our losses, and fear to protect ourselves from danger. It's only when these feelings are denied, so that they cannot be easily and rapidly processed through the system and released, that the situation becomes toxic."*

Candace Pert

Author of *Molecules of Emotion*

(2003)

Controlling these strong emotions can give a child a special "high" in that it allows him or her to understand that he or she can manage their own life in the most appropriate fashion at the most appropriate time.

In summary, to help your CIC solve intense emotional conflicts consider helping your child understand how emotions affect him or her.

Your child should do the following:

➤ Understand the types of situations that

trigger strong emotions.
➤ Make a list of these situations.
➤ Learn to understand the specific type of emotion each situation creates.
➤ Make a list of the most intense emotions.
➤ Prioritize the list by the level of intensity.
➤ Learn how to solve each emotional situation by filling out the emotion charts.
➤ File the charts for future use.

Step 1 Summary for Parents

In the process of assisting your child with the method of solving emotional traumas, you will enhance your own ability to deal with his or her emotions. Help your child cancel the tendency to argue, blame, react emotionally and vindictively:
➤ Learn to make the correct choices in emotionally intense situations.
➤ Understand how to create positive, fun solutions to negative situations.
➤ Appreciate and cultivate the child's creative talents.
➤ Respect the child as a unique individual with unique insights into life.

Step 1 Summary for Teachers
➤ The first and most important action a teacher can take is to "get to know" the child. This requires spending some one-on-one time with the child to learn their unique

strengths, weaknesses, and learning style. Knowing them leads to respecting them. Respect is contagious.

➤ Develop a prearranged hand signal when the child starts getting out of control. Verbal warnings embarrass and threaten the CIC child.

➤ Note the previous Visual Aids section in this chapter.

➤ Work with the Emotions Chart as directed.

➤ Note the previous Anger Management section in this chapter.

"The secret of organization lies in the non-obvious."

Marcus Aurelius

STEP 2

ORGANIZING

"Logic will get you from A to B. Imagination will take you everywhere."

Albert Einstein

Thinking imaginatively is not necessarily an organized process of visualizing life's possibilities. However, with the CIC—slowing him or her down, even momentarily—allows the child to "reflect" upon environmental situations rather than simply apply more emotional energy to a challenging situation.

In order to build organizational limits that help a child focus, it is absolutely essential that supervision and boundaries be established.

A good example of a boundary is a list of rules about how a child needs to behave in the home. For instance, set rules regarding the length of time your child can view TV and play video games. Determine a good time for the child to go to bed, talk on the telephone and communicate with parents or siblings.

Again, society bombards your CIC with hundreds of media images and associated emotions, so the CIC requires daily boundaries. No one can take it all in. Without boundaries, insecurities and tension will arise in your CIC because he or she wants to engage in the media action. Society does not understand the CIC's eagerness to digest it all or the speed of the attempts to do so. Consequently, adults tend to evaluate the child negatively, thinking the child is out of control. Without boundaries, a CIC cannot adequately evaluate his or her life or modify emotional reactions.

Without boundaries a CIC's experiences are like walking into a room where the walls move each time they are touched. A life without boundaries requires a person to be constantly searching for limits without finding them. Boundaries create a sense of security. Boundaries allow your children to focus energy on creative thinking. Boundaries, like walls, need to be firm and constant. If boundaries change regularly, arguments and tension will abound and the child's energy will be spent in conflict.

For instance, if you are having boundary disputes with your child about food intake, particularly foods with sugar, you are asking for trouble, especially when food is often used as a reward or bribe.

In the December 26, 2005, issue of *U.S. News and World Report*, Bernadine Healy, MD, writes, "kids are great manipulators, and parents are much too easily charmed or worn down. Food fights are not fun, and handling them unwisely risks sparking an even fiercer rebellion...but kids will get a balanced diet if their parents manage what's put in the shopping cart, on the kitchen table, and in the lunchbox."

Consequently, if children are out of control and have consumed high amounts of sugar, you do not have a chance of communicating to them. Proper nutrition and diet are essential with all CIC children.

> *"Relying on an artificial form of glucose –sugar –to give us a quick pick-me-up is analogous to, if not as dangerous as, shooting heroin."*

Candace Pert
Author of Molecules of Emotion
(2003)

Imagine a seven-year-old child is running pell-mell through the house and the mother tells the child not to run, or the child will be punished. Is this a limit? No, it is just a warning – no limits or consequences are established. The next day, the child comes home and runs through the house again. This time the mother is busy and doesn't say anything. The child thinks its O.K. to run. The third day, the child comes home and again runs through the house. This time, the mother screams at the child, "How many times have I told you not to run in the house?" Again, it's a confusing message as no significant boundaries are established. In fact, the behavior is reinforced. The fourth day the child comes home and is confused. Should the child run or not? Sometimes the child gets into trouble for running and sometimes not. The parent created the dilemma of the "moving wall," not the child. So what should the parent do?

If, as a parent, you are usually consistent at defining limits and your child still behaves negatively, you need to spend more time developing clear boundaries with them or you will loose the limits battle. Not obeying boundaries is a child's cry for attention. You must find more personalized time for your child. Either way, you will end up giving him or her attention. Without limits, it will be negative time. With limits, the time will more likely be positive. Seek options and establish places and time for certain types of behavior. In the example given, the child and the mother could have developed limits together. A compromise could have been that running outside is acceptable, but running inside is "never" acceptable. Moreover, not adhering to limits has consequences. A possible consequence for the negative behavior could be the loss of TV time. The pros and cons of using television as a vehicle for rewards and punishments will be discussed in a later chapter.

An organized mind and body are the keys of your child's ability to feel secure. If clutter exists, whether it is a confusing instruction or material chaos, the CIC cannot relax and think clearly. Remember these children are action-oriented people; they need to slow down to put life's pieces together. If confused, it is likely that a CIC will argue with you and insist that your limits don't exist, especially if they are not clearly defined. When stressed, the child's problems increase tenfold. To avoid stress, the CIC needs to have clearly identified places for everything in their own room as well as in the mind.

A study by Sara Lazar, assistant in psychology at Massachusetts General Hospital, detailed in the November 2005, issue of *Neuro Report* found the brains of people who meditate were about 5 percent thicker in the areas that deal with focus and memory. Quiet time to think is a kind of meditation that can help your child focus.

To add structure to the home environment, school clothing should be placed in a specific area the night before the school day so the child can find it when he or she wakes up. An organized room means an organized body. As a parent, the most important thing to remember about the CIC is that everything needs a clearly defined designated place. An ordered body facilitates the ability to have an organized mind. A routine or a specified time for each action is a boundary for the successful completion of tasks.

For example, near a door where they enter the house, nail a hook on the wall for coats. Identify a place for shoes and add a table or special area for backpacks and homework, which incidentally will also help the child mentally visualize that the homework needs to be done before the child goes to school. If the coat, shoes, homework and backpack are also beside the door when the child leaves the next day, the whole sequence of body/mind organization is clear. Without these systemized steps, they have no order and panic responses occur instead.

The CIC is usually in a hurry. For instance, he or she might dash into the room to get a pair of socks. If the socks are not in a particular place, the child may start tossing items everywhere in an attempt to find them. This often creates chaos between siblings and parents because many of the things thrown belong to others. One small child can make a whole household upset.

Organizational rules for mind and body will translate to the world around the child and will result in a calmer, more appropriate, happier life for your child, yourself and the rest of the household.

A family "bulletin board" to spread the organizational news helps keep the entire family in line. The bulletin board should detail information for everyone in the family, not just the CIC. Notes with pictures are much better than simply written reminders or parental nagging. When old enough to read and write, let the child make his or her own lists of self-regulatory responsibilities.

Here's an example for a six-year-old child's list:
>Go potty
>Feed the cat
>Wash hands and face
>Eat breakfast
>Bring breakfast dishes to sink
>Get dressed
>Brush hair
>Pick up toys
>Make bed
>Brush teeth

Put on coat and backpack

Time limits are also important. Each task or combination of tasks needs time limits. Time limits are needed to get the CIC to live on schedule with the world.

If the child fails to adhere to the list, the child
should face a "specific consequence" and it is the same
for all family members. Time and structure add a feeling
of security within all children. A good example of a loss
of privilege and its associate time consequence could be
a "time out" or losing five minutes of TV time for various infractions. A chart could be established beside the
TV for the child to record the specific problem, the exact
time it happened and how much TV was missed. The
CIC is especially sensitive to being treated differently
than others; therefore, always treat every sibling the
same.

Be wary of the television, however, television
has little structure; its images are random and frequent.
Therefore, television limits are imperative for children.
Thom Hartmann, author of *The Edison Gene*, corre-
lates television with addictive "substance abuse" such as
cocaine, tobacco, marijuana and alcohol. He says it stimulates chemicals in the brain that changes the brain function and requires more and more "television stimulus" to
meet the addictive, compulsive behavior. At 1000 images
per second, our mind becomes over-stimulated in a short
time and is confused by the data rather than experienc-
ing structure or a sense of order. While educational TV

is an exception, too much of anything can create filtering difficulties in the mind of the CIC. Therefore, using television as a reward and punishment tool helps to build management limits for use of the monster both within the box as well as within the mind of the potential CIC addict.

A focus example: A math teacher saw a child not paying attention in class, so she called on him and asked, "Johnny! What are 2 and 4 and 28 and 44?" Johnny quickly replied, "NBC, CBS, HBO and the Cartoon Network." This is real "addiction!"

Homework and television never work in combination for a CIC. Homework is mind-intensive and TV is body/mind confusing. Homework is a typical stressful situation. The child needs homework structure, time limits, rewards and consequences for missed attention to detail.

Keys to a Structured Life and Homework

Your ultimate goal as a parent is to help your child impose individualized boundaries so he or she can become successful in both the normal everyday world and the world of his or her imagination.

A young CIC requires a lot of consistent monitoring. Gradually, as the child gains control of thinking processes, you can turn over more and more responsibility to him or her. Do not turn the child loose alone before he or she can handle each situation. In other words, do not set the child up for failure. Remember, again, practice makes perfect. Consistent "record keeping" helps you evaluate the learning process and appropriate time to reward and improve the child's behavior.

Always be sure that homework study segments are small enough to allow for a successful finished product. The timer enables managed learning. Timed homework can become a game when the child controls the rules.

Another method of managed homework segments is folding the page in fourths. looking at the whole page sometimes overwhelms children. They may simply refuse to do the homework and not even realize they are over-whelmed. By folding the page, they only see the part of the assignment that is visible – focus equals function. Studying with the timer and a focus helps the child break the homework down into small chunks. Do whatever you need to do to help your child feel in control of all of his or her responsibilities.

If the school repeatedly assigns unreasonable amounts of homework and these management tech-niques do not work, it is time to meet with the teachers and counselors to establish reasonable homework limits.

If the new homework limits still do not work, you may need to consider moving your child to a different school – a private school or charter school – one that is more child-friendly. Some parents even choose to home-school their children. Think out of the box; your child's life is at stake.

If the above program of time organization man-agement does not show any beginning signs of improve-ment after six months, it may be necessary to seek other alternatives or professional help. Talk to the school counselor about his or her management ideas.

In summary, help your child
➤ Enjoy being creative.
➤ Know themselves – strengths and limits.
➤ Evaluate themselves.
➤ By not turning their life over to the school, neighbors, medical profession, or others.
➤ By giving them enough time and love so he or she can feel confident and create solutions to problems.
➤ By being your child's advocate.

Step 2 Summary for the Parents
Provide supportive, consistent discipline so your child will
➤ Have a secure world to operate in.
➤ Learn to create self-imposed limits.
➤ Learn to interact with siblings, friends, schoolmates and parents.

Help your child learn organizational skills by teaching him or her to
➤ Organize the child's room in order to organize the child's mind.
➤ Structure their life for creative visions.
➤ Understand both the limits and the "free" spaces in their world in order to cultivate their imagination.

Help the child understand how much homework needs to be done and in what time limit. A timer or stopwatch could be given to the child to control the amount of homework for each time segment.

➤ Gradually allow your child to plan the time he or she thinks is needed for each homework segment. Estimates of time and task are great management tools.

➤ Decide how many breaks will be necesary between segments to keep the child focused, and to allow him or her to finish all work assignments.

➤ Provide rewards for finishing each segment on time and for finishing all homework.

➤ Place the child in a location free from distractions and one you can easily observe.

Step 2 Summary for the Teachers

➤ Help the CIC child organize their study life by developing an area inside the desk with partitions for each item.

➤ Help the child draw an invisible line around the space at their desk. Emphasis the fact they are not to let their items or feet go beyond this line.

➤ List making (by teacher or child) of things they have to do for class. Parents have to sign it. Provide extra credit or appropriate reward for bringing the signed list to class the next day.

"Life is like riding a bicycle. To keep your balance you must keep moving."

Albert Einstein

STEP 3

"Technological innovation has advanced so rapidly in our lifetime that it has become the primary environmental stimulus responsible for refashioning the animal that began life as Homo...Sapiens. "

Leonard Shlain

The fast-paced, high-tech world we live in requires a moving individual to navigate ever-changing limits. Many leading child psychologists believe that a CIC may have a uniquely adaptive mind that has changed in response to the changing world. The child's mind has adapted to accommodate the accelerating speed of life. Nothing seems to be done slowly today. Everything is calculated in minutes, not days or months of years. The biggest problem for all of us is that society does not focus on the big picture. Most of us are only beginning to understand the impact of technology in our lives. Technological change is happening whether we like it or not and many of yesterdays answers don't work today. Just think about how computers and cellular phones have changed the way we communicate and plan our lives.

Until our schools and society catch up with the speed of this change and its associated information overload, the big question is, "How do you channel your CIC's **fidgety-squirmies**?" How can any child sit still when everything around is moving with the speed of MTV?

The answer could be quite simple. All learning activities should be designed with some type of **movement** to help a CIC acquire quick reactions and think on his or her feet. Using multi-sensory learning activities is the key to a dynamic learning environment. Whether we like it or not, parents and educators are competing with the computer and the TV as teaching "agents" for our child's learning time.

Learning activities for the ever-moving mind could include **Multi-sensory Activities**:

➤ Activities involving the fine motor skills include hands and fingers.

➤ Kinesthetic skills include touching objects with the hands and fingers.

➤ Running, walking and jumping involve the gross motor skills that have to be woven into each day.

➤ Odors and smelling involve the olfactory sense that is also an essential skill in the classroom.

Many of the above activities could be planned into all learning experiences. The CIC is drawn to **action filled situations**. If the learning has the action he or she craves, the child is drawn to the learning. Keep the child busy and he or she will focus the **fidgety squirmies** into creative learning .

Action activities involving all of the child's senses are the key to effective learning. Some good examples of multi-sensory teaching techniques are illustrated on the following pages.

Fine Motor/Kinesthetic Skills

A local school uses the rough feeling of sandpaper cutout letters to activate the kinesthetic sense as children run their fingers over the letters to learn the alphabet.

As they "feel" the letter "B," the students learn how to write the letter and say the sound at the same time.

Auditory Skills

A bottle of water can demonstrate the object that starts with the letter "B." Water coming out of some small-necked bottles makes a "ba" phonetic sound.

Olfactory Skills

The teacher can ask the students what the letter "smells" like. Answers typically will be very creative with small children.

Gross Motor Skills

The teacher can take the children to the playground and have them draw a large letter "B" and hop around the letter. This involves the gross motor skills in the learning activity.

As the alphabet is gradually learned it can also be put into words that apply to the actions. After learning the letters "b," "a" and "t," the children can write the word bat. Putting their name with the letters "b," "a" and "t" they can read "Jason's bat." They also can draw an action picture of the words. As they learn the letter "c," they can read "Jason's cat" – with the letter "m," they can read "Jason's mat." Next, the letter "h" allows them to read "Jason's hat." Other letters can be utilized as they proceed through the alphabet. They can put the pages together and feel the excitement of making their own book complete with illustrations.

Consider that all multi-sensory skills can be combined in each of the above-mentioned environments. For example, sandpaper and other tactile materials can be used to teach all subjects. Everything can be smelled, listened to, marked in the dirt, drawn on concrete and hopped upon.

The above-mentioned exercise utilizes the whole being – fine motor skills, gross motor skills and kinesthetic, visual, auditory and olfactory senses. The learning experience is made for action-oriented children. Moreover, multi-sensory learning is the key to making connections to the students' real world. Remember, as a teacher to always ask the "So what?" question. If you cannot make the real world connection you lose most students.

Computers are also terrific for a CIC because computers involve the fine motor, kinesthetic, visual and auditory skills. A computer is a multi- sensory machine and it enhances learning by also providing structure and creative opportunities. Computers are filtering tools that help creative people scan and organize large amounts of information.

Margaret Mead, renowned anthropologist and author, said that as she studied tribal cultures, she observed that most of the parents used at least three of the child's senses in every learning experience. For their children, learning was a matter of survival. Mead studied many tribal cultures and observed that multi-sensory teaching techniques were used by all of them to impart critical survival skills. We folks from advanced cultures need to do the same. Survival is really the key word for us as well and making connections is what learning is all about.

Jean Houston, an adviser to UNICEF in human and cultural development, said our senses are our "hooks and eyes" that we use to catch information. Continually ask your child what the word feels like, what it smells like or what it moves like. Keep the child thinking creatively and support their visions. There really is not a wrong answer, only a wrong teaching strategy.

Chris Mercogliano, co-director of the Albany Free School in New York, is an example of an administrator with the right attitude about the student as an individual. He says that his school staff considers all children to have unique learning styles and that customizing the child's learning situation is essential for long-term success in school. In the case of a CIC on medication, within weeks of entering the school, the child is off the drugs. Drugs are never considered at the Albany Free School. Even though schools such as this can be expensive, they do have scholarship programs. There is always an open door somewhere. Become the explorer your child is and you'll both find options.

If, however, you are in a situation where you have to stay in the same school and customized learning is not an option, consider applying for Special Education testing, so you can get a legal and binding document called an IEP or Individualized Education Plan. Once a child has an IEP, the school must modify the workload without penalty to your child. The IEP itself is not the complete answer. You still have to work with teach- ers to customize your child's learning in each class. It is a full-time job at first, but it is the only way to win the battle. You can use this IEP as a temporary way to get your child back into the mainstream. Please, don't let the IEP become a permanent crutch. However, think of it like a twisted ankle that takes time to heal. Remember, you will still have to work every day with your child in order to continue to improve his or her homework management skills. Patience is the long-term key to success when using an IEP, but it is still well worth it when your child's future is at stake. For a personal touch to your child's thinking process, attend appropriate movies together. Going to the movies combines the use of action-oriented, auditory and visual senses. The theme of the movie should be one the child can identify with and feel a part of. It's the after-movie sit-down time that is the real creative opportunity. Sitting with your child and interpreting the movie scenes together encourages the child and gets his or her creative juices flowing. As your child learns to segment the pieces of the movie into a setting, plot and message, he or she is actually practicing good homework skills, especially as they apply to English and Social Studies. Eventually, children feel free to think on their own and take pride in their creative insights about abstract experiences. Home video viewing works as well.

Be attentive to the seating issues in movie theaters or in the classroom. The CIC is an aesthetically sensitive learner. The children are little energy sponges that give off and absorb all that is going on around them. Sitting in the middle of a section in the movie theater, as well as in the classroom, may be too confining. The CIC may need to sit near the theater isle or close to the teacher in the classroom. Being close to the teacher encourages the child to think and be alert. like in the movies, the action is right in the child's field of vision.

Front row seating does wonders for attention and concentration in the classroom.

The CIC is very protective of personal space and privacy. Sometimes, personal space represents a larger area than other children. If peers infringe upon the child's space, he or she may react either verbally or physically and even hit the person infringing on his or her energy field. Adults sometimes have a hard time understanding the CIC's reaction. A common school incident occurs when children complain that a CIC hit them when they went up to ask them something. The teacher then asks the CIC if he or she hit another person and the CIC says, "yes," but doesn't know why. The child actually doesn't know why because it is a reflex action. The CIC reacts to invasions of personal space partly because of the response to the intense energy caused by close contact with others. Also, the CIC is defensive due to the years of getting into trouble because of radical physical interactions with peers. Space management is cultural. Understand your student's culture and where their families have originated.

Step 3 Summary for Parents
- ➤ Allow short study homework sessions with movement as necessary
- ➤ Let your child decide the amount of time for each homework segment. Let them set a timer. This helps them focus.
- ➤ Allow your child to have personal space
- ➤ Spend time listening to your child

➤ Work closely with the school so they will understand your child's needs.

Step 3 Summary for Teachers

Provide action-oriented learning for your CIC by involving at least three of the following senses in every learning experience.

➤ Auditory   *hearing* the information

➤ Visual   *seeing* the information

➤ Kinesthetic   *feeling* the information

➤ Olfactory   *smelling* the information

➤ Fine Motor   *touching* the information with the fingers and hands

➤ Gross Motor   *making contact* with the large muscle group such as legs and feet during the learning experience

Accept and appreciate the child's personal space.

➤ Never push or shove the child

➤ Never get in the child's face when talking to them

➤ Regulate, with the help of the parent, where the child sits in the classroom or other crowded spaces

Help the child find the proper learning environment by being aware of his or her special learning styles, special talents and special learning experiences.

"A harmonious life is a life lived at peace with others."

Russ Peterson

STEP 4

coNNecting

"If the less fortunate of us are ashamed of our shabby clothing and shoddy furniture, let's think about what is really important for a moment, and let's be more ashamed of shabby ideas and shoddy philosophies. It would be a sad situation if the wrapper were better than the food wrapped in it."

Albert Einstein

The CIC has **peer-related issues** because of the nature of his or her high activity levels. The child has **difficulty listening, waiting turns and is often impatient with peers** when the child doesn't get his or her way. Consequently, unstructured situations are very difficult. Get the child focused, and he or she is a great thinker! Let the child wander for a moment, and he or she is dancing off the floors, walls and ceilings. Creatively structured situations help curb the child's impulse inclinations and excitement to learn. Consider starting each class with one minute of "at-your-desk stretches" to get active minds focused. Be creative and they will follow.

The CIC gets into trouble on the playground and in the cafeteria more than any other place at school. The main reasons are:

1. The lack of both physical and mental structure on the playground,

2. Desire for action, which creates clashes with peers,

3. The child desires action and excitement, not merely **peer satisfaction**.

Therefore, managed "exercise" is mandatory for the CIC. Stephen Putman, author of *Nature's Ritalin for the Marathon Mind* says nurturing your ADHD child with exercise awakens the scanning minds and calms the senses. His research confirms that exercise affects the brain similar to Ritalin. Exercise the body and mind to respond. Lack of impulse control in unstructured situations often creates chaos between the CIC and peers. Consequently, parents must take the time to inform the school that even at play, their child needs to engage in organized activities.

Cafeteria environments also have students crowded together in tight competitive spaces with a minimum of supervision. Such environments create different challenges of stimulus and restraint behavior for the CIC. Schools could benefit from changing the structure of the cafeteria and playground for all children. For example, teacher aides or appointed child leaders could manage smaller areas of these environments with lines on the floor or chalk on concrete areas. Each environment could contain different types of activities. Relaxing music in the cafeteria can also have a calming effect on kids in general. Research has proven that the mellow music soothes the mind. Classical music in particular has been proven successful in this regard, according to research in similar institutions. Music exercises the brain and the body...breathing more deeply and sitting up straighter.

Lines could be marked on the cafeteria benches, similar to parking spaces, to keep children from being crammed together. Stretching out the lunchroom time between various classes could produce less standing-in-line and more room for each child.

Polite calm communication is absolutely necessary for children with hyperactive minds and bodies. Shouting only stimulates hyperactivity.

> *"Don't criticize your friends till you ride a block on their skateboard."*

Russ Peterson

In the home and at school, parents and teachers have to stress the importance of "appropriate" verbal communication. The CIC should look people directly in the eye when spoken to and when he or she speaks. This gives the CIC inner control of the situation. Eye contact is the only polite way to initiate good communication in general. The CIC needs to learn to state exactly what he or she wants and also recognize they will not always get it. Temper tantrums are a "no, no," as you know.

For example, a CIC must learn to politely say to a peer, "Quincy, it's my turn to play with the ball," instead of grabbing the ball away from Quincy. The CIC prefers to express his or her wishes "physically" instead of verbally because the child is impulse-driven. The CIC thinks it is faster, easier and more efficient to just take the ball. Fortunately, the CIC is a creative thinker. Slow the child down and get him or her to solve problems using thoughtful polite tactics. The child's life will also become mellower.

As mentioned previously, a good end-of-the-day home-based problem solving technique in peer conflicts is to have children act out or role-play their negative interactions. Let your child sleep on it and they will learn. Consider the above situation where the ball was taken with force from a peer. Have the child act out the incident and practice solving the issue. Have the child practice polite responses in private and public situations. If the role-playing is done in a group situation, the group can be called upon to critique the child's compromise solution. Most importantly, it is essential to help your child understand the "positive" results of a compromise in a community of friends. The CIC needs to learn to understand the advantages of becoming more socially acceptable. The child needs help to understand the long-term consequences of both "unacceptable" and "acceptable" behavior."

Often times, the CIC simply does not understand verbal instructions. The child is caught up in the daydream of the moment. Other times, it's as if the instructions just get garbled up inside the mind. The child may need to be physically engaged to understand. As said earlier, short, concise, "polite" instructions always work best for the CIC. For example, say, "Sit down, please," rather than, "Sue, you will need to sit down because you are bothering the other children around you and they cannot concentrate when you are standing there." Being able to focus on the specific moment is the key to a CIC's ability to apply a request for immediate actions.

For all children, especially the CIC, repeatedly clarify whether the child understands your request. After all, consider how difficult it can be to communicate to a significant other. Repetition makes for good communication! Occasionally ask children to repeat the instructions back to you so you can be absolutely certain he or she understood. Do not do this in a way that will embarrass the child—by raising your voice or drawing attention.

Last, but perhaps most importantly, help your child learn to read facial clues or body language. Understanding body language is the key to good social skills for all of us. It is a great way to focus attention and make learning a creative game. Reading facial expressions, body attitudes, "positions" and stances are important in that they allow kids to become adept at thinking through each challenging social interaction in a "reflective" state of mind.

A good exercise to develop body language analysis is to have your child practice emotional faces in a mirror. Ask the child to describe what he or she is feeling as the child looks at their facial expressions. Have the child discuss the face and body language for each emotion. Make it a delightful, action-oriented fun experience. Even consider costumes for both of you and make it theatrical. Always remember to stop, focus and help the child evaluate the body language/emotion correlations quickly. This activity will enable the child to anticipate people's responses and respond in kind, in a creative self-controlled fashion.

Step 4 Summary for Parents

Provide a home environment that encourages precise verbal communication.

➤ Use appropriate situation-specific verbal communications in the home.

➤ Encourage problem-solving analysis of the child's own and other family members body language.

➤ Stress politeness, respect and consideration for all members of family and close associates of the family – everyone in the community is a "window" to your child's behavior.

➤ Practice reading facial clues in the home and discuss the observations.

Step 4 Summary for Teachers

➤ Give the child clear, polite, action-oriented instructions and demand eye contact.

➤ Encourage the child's peers to do the same.
➤ Structure playground and lunchroom CIC child-friendly activities
➤ Role-play disciplinary incidents at appropriate times so CIC students will learn correct procedures.

"The true sign of intelligence is not knowledge but imagination."

Albert Einstein

STEP 5

CREATING

*"The real voyage of discovery
consists not in seeking new lands
but in seeing with new eyes."*

Marcel Proust

An imaginative mind is a problem-solving mind. It searches for unique solutions and delights at the discoveries.

There is nothing like the energy and excitement that can be generated by an imaginative CIC. If this energy could only be bottled and sold, it would be worth millions of dollars. In fact, when it is bottled, it is worth millions. CIC successful adults such as Steven Spielberg, Malcom Forbes, Don Winkler (CEP, Ford Motor Company), David Neeleman (CEO, JetBlue Airlines) and Tom Cruise are representative of this creative class of thinkers who have bottled their energy. A good thing to note is that this energy and excitement is contagious. Help your child realize how talented he or she really is. Now and then, draw comparisons between your child's behavior and people such as those mentioned above. Help the child develop role models to emulate. Everyone needs a superhero in his or her life.

Creative people **daydream** a lot and often have **difficulty focusing** on the moment. They are off scanning the "big picture" ideas of their current circumstances. They are often bored by the mundane. They are active learners and need to be given space to create. A creative thinker does not do well in a box.

While the CIC is a normally positive individual, the child often absorbs negative energy from other people. When the CIC is around negative people, the child also becomes negative. If the child is around positive people, he or she will, in turn, absorb positive energy. This is the case for most of us. As a parent, if you are positive, accepting, happy and loving, your child will also be positive, accepting, happy and loving.

A loving, accepting parent is the key to a CIC's survival. Never "buy into" other people's negative comments or negative opinions about your child. Accepting the child's dynamic interpretation of life helps him or her rise above society's often-negative opinions of your child's active, insightful mind.

*A loving person
lives in
a loving world*

*A hostile person
lives in
a hostile world*

*Everyone you meet
is your mirror*

Ken Keyes, Author

Concentrate your communication on the child's imaginative visions. Thom Hartmann states in *The Edison Gene* that the CIC's distractible nature leads the child to notice "more" in the environment and interpret it in divergent ways. The children see "connections" between the past and the present, their lives and the world and your lives and the future.

The CIC see their world through multi-sensory imaginations. Think of your child as a creative genius, not a "problem child." The child's mind is a treasure to be cultivated not restrained.

Many of the individuals who have shaped the United States of America historically have had some degree of what we now consider CIC characteristics.

Thomas Edison and Albert Einstein are examples of such "change agents." Where would our society be today without them? Cultures change because the extraordinary CIC steps forward and shows the rest of us new perspectives. For example, renowned author Leonard Shlain breaks new ground for the rest of us to digest with glee in his books, *The Alphabet Versus the Goddess and Sex, Time and Power,* where he suggests creative thinkers bridge the time-space continuum and invent new paradigms for life.

David Neeleman, JetBlue Airlines CEO, appeared on *60 Minutes* and told the viewing audience that CIC characteristics were an advantage to his business. (See the glossary for a list of more CIC individuals.) Neeleman stated he had never taken any medication for his CIC personality. In a personal email exchange he stated that his CIC mind had allowed him to "think outside the box" and develop a new management style for his corporation that speaks to changing times and lifestyles of his organization's "creative class."

Another good, everyday example of a unique CIC is a young friend of mine named Jeremy who was diagnosed with CIC at the age of seven. For confidentiality, Jeremy requested his last name and the name of his business be withheld. Jeremy had more than his share of difficulties in school. The school continually contacted his mother because he was not paying attention. He seldom did what he was instructed to do. He was always getting into trouble. When asked how he got into trouble in school, his answer was, "Where do I begin?" He said he ditched school at every opportunity and was about to be expelled. Jeremy's answer to all his "fame" was that he was simply bored in school. In rebuttal to the schools expulsion threat, Jeremy's mother got the school to give him his finals to determine his pass or fail status. Jeremy passed all of his tests without even studying. To keep his mind stimulated, Jeremy had found creative ways to challenge himself. He said he "pushed everything to the edge," challenged the way his teacher's suggested the world was and developed his own visions of reality— especially of himself. He enjoyed **taking risks** such as picking the highest, deepest places to ride into or jump off of with his snowmobile. Early in his school life, his teachers responded to his risk-taking and school difficulties by saying he should be put on Ritalin, but his mother and his aunt supported him and refused. Good Mom!

His aunt had been a school psychologist and did not think medication was the answer. Instead of medication, they encouraged Jeremy to seek his own sources of stimulation. His mom always respected his viewpoints. Jeremy, in turn, learned to respect himself. He said his "school mistakes" turned out to be his learning opportunities.

Jeremy's viewpoint about drug use was substantiated by Dr. Leonard Shlain, a medical doctor associated with California Pacific Medical Center in San Francisco and the University of California at San Francisco. Dr. Shlain is the author of three critically acclaimed, national best selling books about the adaptive human mind. He stated in a speech at the 2005 Conference on World Affairs in Boulder, Colorado, that the myelination, or a protection around the neurons in a child's brain, does not become complete until the ages of 12 to 20. Without the myelinated covering protecting the neurons, Dr. Shlain fears the young minds may be damaged by drug use. He states that long-term studies have not been done on the effects of Ritalin. The *PDR, Physicians'Desk Reference,* also states that long-term studies have not been done on Ritalin. Dr. Shlain believes that common sense goes a long way towards concluding that drug use to control children's behavior is irresponsible. To take the discussion a step further, some experts say that child suicide can be correlated with drug use of any kind. The whole issue of drug use for children is debatable enough that it should just be avoided. Moreover, it is also a fact that drugs that were once considered safe by the medical community are now being pulled from the market because they have been found to have long-term consequences for normal and especially ADD kids.

To complicate the issue even more, consider what former U.S. Drug Enforcement Agency official Gene Haislip says about the debate over Ritalin. His attempt to have a balanced debate about the issue "is an aching reminder of a 'moral' battle" he fought—and lost—"with big drug companies." The pharmaceutical companies contributed $674,000 in fiscal year 2002-2003 to Children With Attention Deficit Disorders or CHADD. It is the largest national association affiliated with ADHD research and has support associations in

almost every state. Given the source of these contribu-
tions, it is no wonder that CHADD members believe that
drugs are an answer to ADD. Kelly Hearn, a journalist
for Alternet, a syndicated press service, says many of the
leading authors of medical literature about ADD, includ-
ing Dr. Russell Barkley, author of Attention Deficit
Hyperactivity Disorder, have admitted to accepting
money from pharmaceutical companies. How, with this
obvious "influence peddling," could one give credibility
to their opinions? **(www.alternet.org/story/20594)**

Returning to Jeremy's story, thanks to a deter-
mined and supportive mother and aunt who did not put
caps on his thinking, Jeremy lived through his early
school years. He did not take any medication and he is
a creative, healthy CIC survivor. This is only one in a
long list of drug-free survivors. Jeremy suggests that it
was his free-ranging creative mind and active body that
enabled him to become a professional hockey player
and later a successful businessman. He found a career
that loved his active mind and body. All CIC can do the
same— acceptance of self and by others is all it takes.
Jeremy, now in his thirties, contributes his spare time to
coaching hockey for a local high school boys' team. He
encourages his athletes to celebrate their "uniqueness,"
just as he did. He tells them to avoid behavior modifica-
tion drugs at all costs in order to preserve their imaginative view of every possibility.

Step 5 Summary for Parents

To maximize creativeness in your CIC:

➤ Investigate all choices your child makes.

➤ Be your child's advocate.

➤ Decide together what the best decisions are and celebrate them.

➤ Stand against negative forces you encounter in your child's life.

➤ Help your child acknowledge mistakes and learn from them—failure is an opportunity to learn and improve.

Encourage your child to associate with positive people:

➤ Invite positive friends to your house to play.

➤ Volunteer your time in age-appropriate organizations that your child would like to be associated with.

➤ Never let negative opinions of others affect your positive opinions of your child.

➤ Draw comparisons between your child and other CIC creative role models.

Appreciate your child's creative mind:

➤ Tell the child every time you notice a spark of creativity.

➤ Celebrate the "golden moments" of imagination by putting symbols the child has created on the wall, bulletin board and refrigerator.

➤ Share all positive statements from others

about your child with him or her and
honor the child's brilliance.

Step 5 Summary for Teachers

➤ Encourage and reward positive attitudes
in the classroom.

➤ Encourage and reward creativity in the
classroom.

➤ Create a grading system that gives points
for positive classroom interactions.

Summary

"Learn from yesterday, live for today, hope for tomorrow. The important thing is not to stop questioning."

Albert Einstein

"The world and its children are perfect the way they are. It's how we often see them that's imperfect."

Jaydene Morrison

This book is written for parents and teachers who look at the world through the creative lens of their children's minds. Parents have the ultimate responsibility to diagnose, evaluate and encourage the "creative inclinations" of their CIC.

It is time we all wake up and see through the questionable opinions and practices about how the CIC need to be "treated." Today, the educational system wants to educate the "normal" child, not the "rebel" such as Jeremy or creative thinkers such as Leonard Schlain. Treasure your creative child. Jeremy's mother did just that, and so did the parents of the other children referred to in this book. Look at the results! The world cannot survive without these children because they are our visionaries.

Clearly all children are unique beings and should not be labeled or expected to act like all other children. In time, your CIC will show you how to appreciate the world through his or her eyes.

Reconsider the main points of each of the five steps in this CIC management guide:

Step 1: THRIVING

Your child should do the following:
➤ Understand the types of situations that trigger strong emotions.
➤ Make a list of these situations.
➤ Learn to understand the specific type of emotion each situation creates.
➤ Make a list of the most intense emotions.
➤ Prioritize the list by level of intensity.
➤ Learn how to solve each emotional situation by filling out Emotion Charts.
➤ File the charts for future use.

For Parents
In the process of assisting your child with the method of solving emotional traumas, you will enhance your own ability to deal with his or her emotions. Help your child cancel his or her tendency to argue, blame, and react emotionally
and vindictively.

➤ Learn to make the correct choices in emotionally intense situations.

➤ Understand how to create positive solutions out of negative situations.

➤ Appreciate and cultivate the child's talents by being positive.

➤ Respect the child as a unique individual with unique insights.

For Teachers

➤ The first and most important action a teacher can take is to "get to know" the CIC child. This requires spending some one-on-one time with the child to learn their unique strengths, weaknesses, and learning style. Knowing them leads to respecting them. Respect is contagious.

➤ Develop a prearranged hand signal when the child starts getting out of control. Verbal warnings embarrass and threaten the CIC child.

➤ Work with the Emotions Chart as directed.

➤ Note the Anger management section in Step 1 Thriving

Step 2: ORGANIZING

In summary, **Help Your Child:**

➤ Enjoy being creative.

➤ Know themselves – strengths and limits.

➤ Evaluate themselves.

➤ Do not turn the child's life over to the school, neighbors, medical profession, or others.

➤ Give the child enough time and love to feel confident enough to create his or her own solutions to problems.

➤ Be your child's advocate.

➤ Learn to interact with siblings, friends, schoolmates and adults.

For Parents

Provide supportive, consistent discipline so your child will:

➤ Have a secure world to operate in.

➤ Learn to create self-imposed limits.

Help your child learn organizational skills by teaching the child to:

➤ Organize their room in order to organize their mind

➤ Structure their life for creative visions

➤ Understand both the limits and the "free" spaces in the child's world in order to cultivate his or her imagination.

Help the child understand how much homework needs to be done and in what time limit:

➤ A timer or stopwatch could be given to the child to control the amount of homework for each time segment.

➤ Gradually allow your child to plan the time

he or she thinks is needed for each home-work segment. Estimates of time and task are great management tools.

➤ Decide how many breaks will be necesary between segments to keep the child focused, and to allow him or her to finish all work assignments.

➤ Provide rewards for finishing each segment on time and for finishing all homework.

➤ Place the child in a location free from distractions and one you can easily observe.

For Teachers

➤ Help the CIC child organize their study life by developing an area inside the desk with partitions for each item.

➤ Help the child draw an invisible line around his space at their desk. Emphasis the fact they are not to let their items or feet go beyond this line.

➤ List making (by teacher or child) of things they have to do for class.

➤ Parents have to sign all lists. Give extra credit or appropriate reward for bringing the signed list to class the next day.

Step 3: MOVING

For Parents

➤ Allow short study homework sessions with movement as necessary

➤ Let your child decide the amount of time for each homework segment. Let them set a timer. This helps them focus.

➤ Allow your child to have personal space

➤ Spend time listening to your child

➤ Work closely with the school so they will understand your child's needs.

For Teachers

Provide action-oriented learning for your student by involving three of the following senses in every learning experience:

➤ Auditory   *hearing* the information

➤ Visual   *seeing* the information

➤ Kinesthetic   *feeling* the information

➤ Olfactory   *smelling* the information

➤ Fine Motor   *touching* the information with the fingers and hands

➤ Gross Motor   *making contact* with the large muscle group such as legs and feet during the learning experience

Accept and appreciate your student's personal space:

➤ Never push or shove the student

➤ Never get in the child's face when talking

➤ Regulate, with the help of the child's parent, where the child sits in the classroom and who he or she interacts with

Help the CIC student find the proper learning environment by being aware of special talents and learning styles as well as special likes and dislikes.

Step 4: CONNECTING

For Parents

Provide a home environment that encourages precise verbal communication:

➤ Use appropriate situation-specific verbal communications in the home.

➤ Encourage problem-solving analysis of the child's own and other family members body language.

➤ Stress politeness, respect and consideration for all members of the family and close associates of the family – everyone in the community is a "window" to your child's behavior.

➤ Practice reading facial clues in the home and discuss the observations.

For Teachers

➤ Give the CIC student clear, action-oriented instructions and demand eye contact.

➤ Encourage the child's peers to do the same.

➤ Structure playground and lunchroom CIC child-friendly activites.

➤ Role-play disciplinary incidents at appropriate times so CIC students will learn correct procedures.

Step 5: CREATING

To maximize creativeness in your CIC:
- Investigate all choices your child makes.
- Be your child's advocate.
- Decide together what the best decisions are and celebrate them.
- Stand against negative forces you encounter in your child's life.
- Help your child acknowledge mistakes and learn from them – failure is an opportunity to learn and improve.

Encourage your child to associate with positive people:
- Invite positive friends to your house to play.
- Volunteer your time in age-appropriate organizations that your child would like to be associated with.
- Never let negative opinions of others affect your positive opinions of your child.
- Draw comparisons between your child and other CIC creative role models.
- Appreciate your child's creative mind
- Tell the child every time you notice a spark of creativity.
- Celebrate the Golden Moments by putting items the child has created on the wall, bulletin board and refrigerator—celebrate every moment.

➤ Share all positive statements from others about
   your child with him or her and
   honor the child's brilliance.

For Teachers

➤ Encourage and reward positive attitudes
   in the classroom.
➤ Encourage and reward creativity in the
   classroom.
➤ Create a grading system that gives points
   for positive classroom interactions.

In conclusion, these management techniques should
be practiced until your child or student is managing his
or her own life with relative ease. When this point happens, it clearly varies per child. If you begin the process
early, when your child or student is four or five-years-
old, by middle school the child or student should be on
his or her own. However, occasional monitoring by you
and your child or student needs to be practiced throughout those high-energy years of middle school. In many
cases, the challenge can be difficult—as in the early
days in elementary school. The practice of self-charting
is a great skill for the child to use. Most of the analysis
in these later years can occur in the head. No paper is
needed.

You may recognize that you are already practicing
some versions of the methods mentioned in this management guide. Great! Keep it up! You and the child are,
therefore, walking hand in hand into a delightful future.

Mutual commitment is a partnership that results in a successful route to cultivating the creative mind.

For further questions and to receive a bimonthly

newsletter, email the author, Jaydene Morrison, at

MorEducate@gmail.com

GLOSSARY

E M O T I O N S   C H A R T

Event _____

Emotion(s) felt _____

_____

People involved _____

_____

Place incident happened

_____

Actions involved _____

_____

Trigger situation –or– event that started problem

_____

Consequence of behavior

_____

Potential solutions _____

_____

Future steps

_____

_____

FAMOUS PEOPLE WITH ADD

With Perseverance They Made It – So Can You!

Hans Christian Anderson

Ann Bancroft

Beethoven

Harry Belafonte

Alexander Graham Bell

Gregory Boyington

Wright Brothers

Sir Richard Francis Burton

George Bush's Children

Admiral Richard Byrd

Thomas Carlyle

Andres Carnegie

Lewis Carroll

Prince Charles

Cher

Agatha Christie

Winston Churchill

John Corcoran

Tom Cruise

Leonardo da Vinci

Salvador Dali

Walt Disney

Thomas Edison

Albert Einstein

Dwight D. Eisenhower

Michael Faraday

F. Scott Fitzgerald

Malcom Forbes

Henry Ford

Benjamin Franklin

Zsa Zsa Gabor

Galileo

Danny Glover

Tracey Gold

Whoopi Goldberg

Stephen Hawking

Handel

William Randolph Hearst

Ernest & Mariel Hemingway

Dustin Hoffman

Bruce Jenner

"Magic" Johnson

Michael Jordan

John F. Kennedy

Robert Kennedy

Jason Kidd

John Lennon

Carl Lewis

Abraham Lincoln

Greg Louganis

James Clerk Maxwell

Steve McQueen

Mozart

David H. Murdock

Napoleon

Nasser

Isaac Newton

Jack Nicholson

Nostradamus

Luci Baines Johnson Nugent

Louis Pasteur

General George Patton

Picasso

Edgar Allan Poe

Puccini

Sergei Rachmaninoff

Buddy Rich

Eddie Rickenbacker

Joan Rivers

Nelson & John D. Rockefeller

Rodir

Pete Rose

Eleanor Roosevelt

Anwar Sadat

Babe Ruth

Nolan Ryan

Pierre Salinger

Charles Schwab

George C. Scott

George Bernard Shaw

Tom Smothers

Socrates

Suzanne Somers

Sylvester Stallone

Jackie Stewart

James Stewart

Thomas Thoreau

Henry David Thoreau

Leo Tolstoy

Alberto Tomba

Van Gogh

Russell Varian

Jules Verne

Werner von Braun

Lindsay Wagner

General Westmoreland

Weyerhauser Family

Russell White

Robin Williams

Woodrow Wilson

Henry Winkler

Stevie Wonder

F.W. Woolworth

Wrigley

William Butler Yates

Compiled by:

A.D.D. OF MID-PENINSULA
Sheridan Avenue
Suite 339
Palo Alto, CA 94306-2020

About the Author

Jaydene Morrison, **MS, LPC, NCSP, NCC** _is_ _the author of_ Coping with ADD/ADHD _and co-author of_ Coping with Learning Disabilities. _Both books have been printed in hardback and paperback editions._

She is a school psychologist and mental health therapist. For the past 35 years, she has worked in many school systems throughout the United States. Morrison has been a classroom teacher, special education instructor and school counselor and has also held administrative positions. She has completed 114 additional graduate hours beyond her Master's Degree.

Morrison led the earlier Special Education Area by creating the first Resource Room concept in the state of Oklahoma. She has worked with ADD/ADHD adults and children and has trained teachers and administrators to work with ADD/ADHD individuals.

She resides in the mountains of Colorado.

Printed in the United States
60155LVS00005B/310-330

9 781425 920296